Three Sonatas for Pianoforte with Violin

Recent Researches in Music

A-R Editions publishes seven series of critical editions, spanning the history of Western music, American music, and oral traditions.

Recent Researches in the Music of the Middle Ages and Early Renaissance
    Charles M. Atkinson, general editor

Recent Researches in the Music of the Renaissance
    James Haar, general editor

Recent Researches in the Music of the Baroque Era
    Christoph Wolff, general editor

Recent Researches in the Music of the Classical Era
    Eugene K. Wolf, general editor

Recent Researches in the Music of the Nineteenth and Early Twentieth Centuries
    Rufus Hallmark, general editor

Recent Researches in American Music
    John M. Graziano, general editor

Recent Researches in the Oral Traditions of Music
    Philip V. Bohlman, general editor

Each edition in *Recent Researches* is devoted to works by a single composer or to a single genre. The content is chosen for its high quality and historical importance, and each edition includes a substantial introduction and critical report. The music is engraved according to the highest standards of production using the proprietary software MusE, owned by Music|Notes.™

For information on establishing a standing order to any of our series, or for editorial guidelines on submitting proposals, please contact:

A-R Editions, Inc.
801 Deming Way
Madison, Wisconsin 53717

800 736-0070 (U.S. book orders)
608 836-9000 (phone)
608 831-8200 (fax)
http://www.areditions.com

RECENT RESEARCHES IN THE MUSIC OF THE NINETEENTH AND EARLY TWENTIETH CENTURIES, 27

George Frederick Pinto

Three Sonatas for Pianoforte with Violin

Edited by Linda W. Perry

A-R Editions, Inc.

Madison

A violin part is available from the publisher.

A-R Editions, Inc., Madison, Wisconsin 53717
© 1999 by A-R Editions, Inc.

All rights reserved. No part of this book may be reproduced or transmitted in any form by any electronic or mechanical means (including photocopying, recording, or information storage and retrieval) without permission in writing from the publisher.

The purchase of this work does not convey the right to perform it in public, nor to make a recording of it for any purpose. Such permission must be obtained in advance from the publisher.

A-R Editions is pleased to support scholars and performers in their use of *Recent Researches* material for study or performance. Subscribers to any of the *Recent Researches* series, as well as patrons of subscribing institutions, are invited to apply for information about our "Copyright Sharing Policy."

Printed in the United States of America

ISBN 0-89579-430-6
ISSN 0193-5364

♾ The paper used in this publication meets the minimum requirements of the American National Standard for Information Sciences—Permanence of Paper for Printed Library Materials, ANSI Z39.48-1984.

Contents

Acknowledgments vi

Introduction vii
  The Composer vii
  Historical Background vii
  The Music of the Edition viii
  Notes on Performance ix
  Notes xii

Plates xiv

Sonata No. 1 in G Minor 1
  Allegro moderato con espressione 1
  Adagio 14
  Rondo: Allegretto grazioso 19

Sonata No. 2 in A Major 35
  Allegro moderato con espressione 35
  Andante 49
  Rondo: Allegro con brio 52

Sonata No. 3 in B-flat Major 70
  Allegro moderato con espressione con spirito 70
  Adagio affettuoso e con sentimento 82
  Rondo: Allegro moderato 86

Critical Report 99
  Source 99
  Editorial Methods 99
  Critical Notes 99

Appendix: An Embellished Version of the Adagio of Sonata No. 1 101

Acknowledgments

I would like to express my great appreciation to Dr. Nicholas Temperley for introducing me to the works of Pinto and for his continued guidance, encouragement, interest, and invaluable expertise throughout this project. The plates from the 1806 edition were photographed from a copy in Dr. Temperley's possession with his kind permission. David Perry's support has also been essential, as he has answered numerous violinistic questions and has performed the sonatas with me.

Introduction

The Composer

The English composer George Frederick Pinto (born 25 September 1785, died 23 March 1806) was described in superlative terms by some of his most distinguished contemporaries. Samuel Wesley (1766–1837) stated that "a greater musical genius has not been known," and William Ayrton (1777–1858) remarked that some of his compositions "would do credit to the name of the greatest composer who ever lived." Johann Peter Salomon (1745–1815), his violin teacher and a leading London concert manager, felt that if he had not died at such an early age, "England would have had the honour of producing a second Mozart."[1]

While it seems likely that his youthful precocity and his untimely death at the age of twenty may have combined to produce this very high esteem in his contemporaries, modern scholars approaching his work with greater objectivity have also found it worthy of their attention. Alexander L. Ringer refers to him as "the most daring representative" of the London Pianoforte School, a "prophet of keyboard things to come" who "thought pianistically in the nineteenth-century sense from the very outset." Nicholas Temperley, whose modern editions of Pinto's piano music and songs have made this music available to contemporary performers and audiences, calls his music "a bright light in a dark hour of English music," while William S. Newman points to his wide range of musical thinking and feeling, remarkable for such a young composer.[2]

Little is known about Pinto's short life or about the circumstances of his death. His maternal grandfather, Thomas Pinto, was an Italian-born violinist who emigrated to England. His father, Samuel Saunders, died young and apparently played little role in his life. He used his mother's last name. Raised by his mother, Julia Pinto, and his step-grandmother, Charlotte Brent (Thomas Pinto's second wife), who was a singer, he proved to be precocious at an early age as a violinist, pianist, and composer. He studied violin with Salomon and was presented in concerts as early as 1796. He also became an accomplished pianist, performing as both violinist and pianist at concerts in London, Edinburgh, and possibly Paris until 1804, when his health began to deteriorate.

The medical cause of Pinto's death remains obscure, attributed in most accounts to "dissipation." Salomon, his teacher, speaks of his inability to "resist the allurements of society."[3] Pohl in *Grove's Dictionary* refers to his health, "undermined by excesses," and Sainsbury's *Dictionary* in 1825 calls him a "martyr to dissipation." *Baker's Biographical Dictionary* mentions his "sexual indulgence and general dissipation."[4]

Although George Pinto never knew his grandfather, who died before George was born, accounts of the two men indicate similar precocity and temperament. Sainsbury's *Dictionary* refers to Thomas Pinto's violinistic prowess but comments that "he was very idle, inclining more to the fine gentleman than the musical student" (p. 294). Accounts of contemporaries attribute the same qualities to the younger Pinto. However, Temperley points out that the extent of his performance and compositional activities "seems to give the lie to the frequent stories of his idleness and dissipation. He must have been an extraordinarily fast worker."[5]

Pinto's works enjoyed popularity during and immediately following his brief life but soon slipped into obscurity. Some of his manuscripts were edited and published after his death by Samuel Wesley, and there was a brief attempt to revive some works in the 1840s. Those that survive include songs, pieces for solo keyboard, violin duets, and sonatas for keyboard and violin. The solo keyboard sonatas have been highly acclaimed, and Alexander Ringer even ventures to hint at a possible influence on Beethoven. Thanks to the efforts of Nicholas Temperley, scholarly editions of the solo keyboard works are now available in *The London Pianoforte School*. Several of the songs, also edited by Temperley, may be found in *Musica Brittanica*. Until now, however, there were no modern editions of the sonatas for keyboard and violin.[6] The "Three Sonatas for the Pianoforte with an Accompaniment for a Violin" were among Pinto's last compositions, published by his mother after his death in 1806.

Historical Background

London in the last decades of the eighteenth century was an international musical center, with musicians of many nationalities living and working there. It was particularly a center of pianistic virtuosity, as the English were developing the world's leading pianoforte industry. The English piano around 1800 was noted for its sonority and brilliance, in comparison with the Viennese piano, favored for its delicacy and clarity of articulation. The music publishing industry was also thriving in London, encouraging prolific composition.

The large group of virtuoso pianists and composers, both native and foreign, who were prominent in London during this period have come to be known as the London Pianoforte School. The acknowledged leader of this school was Muzio Clementi (1752–1832), known in his own time as the "father of the pianoforte."[7] The Italian-born Clementi spent most of his life in England and was actively involved in performing, teaching, composing, publishing, and the pianoforte manufacturing industry, exerting a strong influence on all aspects of English pianism.

Other prominent members of the group included immigrants J. C. Bach, J. L. Dussek, and J. B. Cramer, as well as native-born John Field, Samuel Wesley, and George Pinto. They were widely respected on the Continent more for their pianism (both their technical flair and their expressivity) than for their compositions, although most were also prolific composers. This may account for the fact that among their works, the studies and instruction books gained the greatest acceptance.

In addition to the musicians in residence, London played host to many outstanding performers and composers from the Continent. Haydn made London tours in 1791–92 and 1794–95, arranged by Salomon, and wrote his mature piano trios there. Hummel and Pleyel also concertized there in the 1790s.

While the London composers did not achieve first-rank prominence, there was much that was innovative in their style. As Sandra P. Rosenblum notes, Clementi "developed an expressive legato style of composition and performance for which he and his followers became widely known."[8] Dussek and Field in particular displayed early romantic characteristics which were developed later in the nineteenth century by other composers. Among Pinto's works, the second of the three sonatas presented in this edition could be said to foreshadow the style of Schubert.

The Music of the Edition

Pinto's sonatas are of the "accompanied keyboard" type which flourished, particularly in amateur circles, in the latter part of the eighteenth century and the early years of the nineteenth. From 1760 to 1785, this was the most commonly published type of sonata, with most composers embracing the genre, including J. C. Bach, C. P. E. Bach, Clementi, Dussek, and Hummel.[9] They must have been extremely popular in London in Pinto's time, judging from the output of the composers of the London Pianoforte School. Dussek alone wrote eighty-six sonatas in this genre, and nearly half of Cramer's total output of 124 sonatas were accompanied.[10] Mozart's first six sonatas for keyboard and violin (or flute), K. 10–15, influenced by Johann Schobert's accompanied sonatas, were written at age eight and published in London in 1765.

Many of these sonatas, including all those of Haydn, were self-sufficient keyboard sonatas with an optional part for another "accompanying" instrument, usually the violin. Others provided greater degrees of participation by the violin, whose involvement reached true equality with the pianoforte in the mature sonatas of Mozart. Primarily written for amateurs, the sonatas were easily accessible to both performer and listener and could provide a pleasant evening of home entertainment. Generally they were lighter and more popular in character than the more serious solo sonatas of the same composers. In the nineteenth century, as chamber music went to the concert stage and into the realm of professional musicians, the "amateur" variety declined in popularity. Czerny was among the last to write the "accompanied keyboard" type of sonata.

Pinto follows a middle road in treatment of the two instruments, allowing the violin a substantial role in presenting thematic material but giving the bulk of the technical display to the pianoforte. The violinist of today, who may not be accustomed to thinking of himself as the accompanist in a duo situation, may feel somewhat shortchanged in terms of the number of notes he is assigned to play.

Formally, Pinto's three sonatas follow a rather conventional plan. All are in a three-movement fast-slow-fast sequence, with an opening sonata-allegro movement in $\frac{4}{4}$ meter and a final $\frac{2}{4}$ rondo. The slow movements of the first and third sonatas are in ternary form, and that of the second is rounded binary.

The first sonata, in G minor, is overall the strongest of the three and comes closest to equal treatment of the two instruments throughout. While the violin gets its fair share of thematic material, the piano gets the *Sturm und Drang* technical displays. The first movement is the only one of all the sonatas in a minor mode and is also the only one which allows the violin to present the opening theme. It contains the most passionate writing of any of the sonatas, with chromatic sequences and angular themes. The second movement, in E-flat major, is eloquently expressive for each instrument and allows for considerable embellishment of both parts. The third is a rather elaborate rondo in G major with a genial primary subject and more serious internal sections. It includes two fugato developmental sections, one of which returns to the G-minor intensity of the opening movement, and a written-out cadenza for the piano. This is the most complex of the three rondos, both formally and harmonically, but it suffers from overuse of the dotted rhythmic motive. It is the only movement within which Pinto changes key signatures (three times, to G minor, E-flat major, and D major).

The second sonata, in A major, is the most lyrical of the three, Schubertian in character. The first movement is particularly attractive, genial rather than dramatic, with an abundance of gently curving, amiable melodies. Its second movement is the least inspired, both melodically and harmonically, but it can be enhanced by tasteful embellishment of the repetitions. The final rondo is sprightly and full of good humor, although rhythmically repetitive. Given a spirited performance, it is a very effective finale.

The first movement of the third sonata, in B-flat major, is not as imaginative thematically as those of the other two sonatas and places the violin in a more subsidiary role. The second movement, in G-flat major, contains sustained, expressive writing similar to that of the first sonata, with a dark, dramatic middle section in E-flat minor for the piano alone. There are some awkward pauses which might be judiciously filled in by the performers, and embellishment of the return of the "A" section will enhance its effect. The very attractive final movement is a good-natured rondo with some unexpected harmonic twists. The violin is an equal partner throughout, having for the first time in these sonatas a bit of thematic material (in the "B" sections) which is not shared with the piano.

The quality of composition spans a wide range in the accompanied keyboard sonatas of the eighteenth and nineteenth centuries. Many are truly forgettable works. However, Pinto's sonatas, while uneven at times, are attractive works that deserve to be rediscovered and played today, with some movements representative of the best writing to come from the London Pianoforte School.

Notes on Performance

A historically accurate performance of music of this period requires some knowledge of performance practices of the time. A summary of applicable practices follows here, based on treatises of the period and on more recent scholarly research concerning those practices. Individual sonatas are indicated by Roman numerals, movements by Arabic numerals.

Articulation and Touch

Both C. P. E. Bach in 1752 and Türk in 1789 described non-legato as the basic touch for keyboard music and stated that passages which did not indicate either a slur or some sort of staccato should be played non-legato. Bach was specific in assigning half the value of the note in non-legato passages, but Türk and Marpurg considered that too short, reducing the value only by one-eighth to one-fourth. Türk did not revise this advice in his 1802 edition, despite the evidence that legato was by then the prevailing practice.[11]

Clementi in 1801 called legato the prevailing touch: "When the composer leaves the legato and staccato to the performer's taste, the best rule is to adhere chiefly to the legato, reserving the staccato to give spirit occasionally to certain passages, and to set off the higher beauties of the legato." He developed this touch after the time of Mozart, on the improved English pianos. Dussek, Clementi, and his students, Cramer and Field, were said to be admired for their cantabile legato style.[12]

It is important to note that the custom of writing successive measure-length slurs, each terminating at the barline, was a carryover from string bowing notations and does not necessarily mean to discontinue the legato at each barline. While short slurs usually indicate a shortened release of the last note, longer slurs are more ambiguous and should be considered according to the context.

It should not be assumed that slurs and bowing indications are synonymous. While slurred notes should generally be played with one bow, unslurred notes (even those marked with dots or strokes) are not necessarily to be played with alternate bows. Leopold Mozart speaks of those composers who clumsily notate the style of a performance and states that in such cases "everything depends on the good judgment of the violinist."[13]

With regard to strokes and dots, Türk (p. 342) states that they have the same meaning but indicates that others consider the stroke to be shorter than the dot. He cautions that staccato notes should be sustained longer in slow tempos than in fast.

Both Quantz[14] and Mozart (p. 45) say that slurs over dotted notes indicate they should be played with one bow, without detaching the notes but articulating with pressure of the bow. Mozart further explains that strokes with slurs over them are to be played on one bow, but detached from one another. Georg Simon Löhlein (1774) later states that dots under slurs should be detached.[15]

By 1801 Clementi (p. 8) made a clear differentiation between strokes, dots, and slurred dots. Strokes are shortest, dots less staccato, and slurred dots still less staccato. Again, the degree of shortness is determined by the speed and character of the piece.

While many theorists of the period agreed with Clementi, in actual practice composers were rather careless in their penmanship and inconsistent in their use of the markings. Pinto in II-2 used all three markings in parallel situations, indicating that he was not particularly concerned with differentiations.

Dynamics and Balance

In playing music of this period, the performer should keep in mind that the pianoforte had a considerably more limited dynamic range than the modern grand piano. Early composers for the pianoforte used dynamic markings sparsely, usually limited to *p* and *f*, with gradations within the sections left to the discretion of the performer.

On the other hand, the modern violin and bow that we know today were well established by 1800. Indeed, the most sought-after violins of today date from the early eighteenth century in Italy, and the contour of the modern bow was established around 1785 by François Tourte. However, there were some differences in the fittings of that time. The bridge was probably a little lower and less arched than the modern bridge, the neck and fingerboard slightly shorter, and gut strings were used. Around 1800, the fittings were altered to approximately their present state to facilitate playing in the highest positions, to compensate for the increased tension of a higher concert pitch, and to give a more powerful and brilliant sound.[16]

This relative difference in volume of the two instruments probably accounts for much of the scoring. While the piano has the bulk of the passage work, its accumulated sound on the pianoforte would not have offered the relatively stronger violin much competition. On the modern grand, the more resonant sound can easily overbalance the violin. Most of the violin writing is in the lower range of the instrument, with no attempt to exploit its more brilliant upper range to compete with the keyboard.

Often there is no opening dynamic indicated. Johann Rellstab in 1790 and Heinrich Koch in 1802 indicated that forte was the prevailing dynamic level in fast tempi when no indication was written, the degree dependent on the nature of the movement.[17] Türk writes of the necessity of adapting the degree of loudness to the sentiments expressed (p. 339).

Pinto uses *p, f, ff,* and occasionally *pp, cresc., dim.,* and hairpins. *Fz* and *sf* are frequent and apparently interchangeable. Only one of his fast movements (I-1) has an opening dynamic (*p*). *Dolce,* used frequently by Pinto in his *allegro* movements, is related to dynamics. Clementi defines it thus: "sweet, with taste, now and then swelling some notes" (p. 9). Used at the beginning of the second and third sonatas, it implies a quiet beginning. The other fast movements, containing no indications, might be appropriately begun *forte.*

Pedal

Pinto's sonatas have no pedal indications, although the English pianos had damper pedals, and pedal indications had begun to appear in other English editions and in Beethoven's works by this time. Written indications were usually to denote special effects, with conventional uses left to the discretion of the performer.[18] Sparing use of the pedal for coloristic effects, avoiding blurring of harmonies, would seem appropriate in Pinto's sonatas.

Tempo

Tempo markings indicate both the tempo and the character of the music. *Allegro* literally means "cheerful" or "spirited" but has traditionally been associated with "fast" movements. The actual speed of an "allegro" movement is tempered by several factors: the time signature ($\frac{2}{4}$ or $\frac{3}{8}$ will be faster than $\frac{4}{4}$), the shortest note values, the harmonic rhythm, and other words and phrases in the tempo directive.

Each of Pinto's five *allegro* movements is tempered by one or more qualifying words: *con espressione, con brio, con spirito, moderato.* Clementi (p. 14) defines *con espressione* thus: "with expression; that is, with passionate feeling, where every note has its peculiar force and energy; and where even the severity of time may be relaxed for extraordinary effects." Clementi, in his ranking of velocity indications, lists *con brio* and *con spirito* higher on the scale than either *allegro* or *vivace. Moderato,* on the other hand, would have a tempering effect on the speed (p. 13).

Allegretto was described by Heinrich Koch (1802) as "noticeably slower than allegro, with less spirited expression and with notes less sharply detached."[19] The players should take note of the *Allegretto grazioso* indication for I-3. Its $\frac{2}{4}$ time signature and spritely rondo theme might tempt a faster tempo, which becomes inappropriate for the inner sections of the movement.

Adagio was considered by Clementi to be the slowest tempo indication. Cramer agreed, while others (Mozart, Hummel, Czerny) considered *grave* the slowest, and Haydn and Beethoven thought *largo* to be slowest.[20] Pinto's *adagios,* coupled with the additional instructions (*sostenuto, affettuoso e con sentimento*), seem to indicate slow tempo and considerable rubato. Given the very long note values, these movements appear to call for embellishment by the performers if these expressive qualities are to be realized within the very slow tempos.

Pinto's frequent use of *lento* for one- or two-bar passages in his *allegros,* usually followed by a *tempo primo* or *a tempo* indication, seems to indicate simply a relaxation of tempo, not a drastic tempo change, similar to the use in the early eighteenth century of *adagio* for a cadence in an *allegro* movement.

Rhythm

The common practice, clearly delineated by C. P. E. Bach and by Türk, of assimilating mixed meters (eighths or dotted rhythms against triplets) in performance comes into question in II-1 and III-1. Although by 1800 composers were notating their preferences more carefully, this type of passage might have been ambiguous well into the nineteenth century. In II-1, measure 58, the left hand should adjust to the final triplet notes of the right hand. However, in III-1, measures 95 and 109, the duple rhythm is related to the character of the first theme and should not be assimilated.

Ornamentation

Trills

Pinto's sonatas contain trills, turns, and various types of small-note ornaments. Clementi (p. 11) wrote in 1801 that "the general mark for the shake is *tr,* and composers trust chiefly to the taste and judgment of the performer, whether it shall be long, short, transient, or turned (with terminating notes)." By 1800 opinion was divided on whether upper or main note starts were preferable, and many composers were notating both starting notes and terminations.

Pinto consistently notates his trills with the sign *tr*. He frequently writes out terminations, and often he notates a trill start from above or below with a small eighth note before the main note. Although it is hazardous to assume consistency in Pinto's markings, a main note start seems appropriate in most of the trills for which he does not specify an upper or lower start. However, many of the trills for which he writes no termination seem to require one. These are notated in brackets.

Turns

Pinto's indications for the turn are puzzling, as instead of the customary ∾, he uses ⸜, the usual sign for the inverted turn. Since in all contexts it appears the normal turn is intended, that symbol has been used in this edition. In only one movement, I-2, Pinto uses an ornament often employed ambiguously by Haydn for either the turn or the mordent, ⨯. In Pinto's case, the ornament, occurring over long tied notes in an *adagio* movement, requires the more melodic turn, not the mordent.

In some instances Pinto writes out turns in small notes (e.g., III-3, m. 122). In other cases he uses the *tr* sign interchangeably with the turn. Two instances of this have been regularized, since they occur in parallel passages. In I-1, measures 25–29, the turn sign is used, but in the parallel measures 146–50, *tr* appears, while in I-3, measures 132 and 134, a trill is followed by a turn. In all these instances, he apparently means a "turned shake," or a brief trill with termination. Given the short amount of time in each case, however, this could mean nothing lengthier than the standard four-note turn, and the trills have therefore been changed to turns (with reports in the critical notes).

Clementi's illustrations of the turn (p. 10, shown below) were standard, although various writers indicated slight rhythmic variants. The turn on the note generally began from above, comprising four notes. The turn "on the dot," or after the note, began on the note and consisted of five notes:

Appoggiaturas and other small-note ornaments

Treatise-writers of the period generally agree that small notes could have a variety of interpretations. The notated value of the small note does not necessarily denote the actual value of the note. The performer must determine not only the length, but also whether to take the value of the small note from the preceding or the following note.

Rosenblum (pp. 21ff.) divides small-note ornaments into three categories: (1) the appoggiatura, which may be either short or long, and takes its value from the following note; (2) the grace note, played before the beat and taking time from the preceding note, but slurred to the following note; (3) the after-note, slurred to the preceding note and taking time from it (called "termination," or *Nachschlag*, by Türk).

Türk cited the difficulty of determining whether appoggiaturas should be played long or short. Long appoggiaturas vary in length in relation to the notes which they precede, while short appoggiaturas are played quickly regardless of the value of the following note. Türk called for composers to write long appoggiaturas in their prescribed note values to avoid this confusion (p. 195). Haydn, Mozart, and others did this increasingly in the last decades of the eighteenth century, while other composers continued the old, ambiguous practices.

All of Pinto's one-note ornaments are indicated as small eighth notes, either slashed or unslashed. In this edition, the two types of eighths have been set as grace notes and appoggiaturas, respectively, since their notation in the source is remarkably consistent both within and between movements: slashed eighths precede principal notes of a quarter-note or lesser value, while unslashed eighths precede notes of a quarter-note or greater value. The only instances where the notation of ornamental eighths has been altered occur in I-3 and have been documented in critical notes. All the unslashed eighths can be appropriately played as short appoggiaturas, except the one in II-3, measure 135, which is long.

In regard to the slashed eighths, Cramer's advice in his 1812 *Instructions for the Pianoforte,* cited by Rosenblum (p. 223), is especially pertinent. He advises playing a short appoggiatura before a group of four sixteenth notes "quick *with* the first note, so as not to break the regularity of the group" (similar to the acciaccatura, in which the main note and appoggiatura are struck simultaneously, and the short note released quickly). In instances such as this, Pinto notates small slashed eighth notes before groups of four sixteenths or triplet groups (see I-1, m. 98; all those in II-1; and III-1, mm. 19 and 147). All other slashed eighths can be played as grace notes, except in III-3, measure 195, which indicates an upper note start of the trill, preferably begun on the beat.

The sonatas also contain a few two- and three-note ornaments which should be played on the beat (e.g., I-3, m. 86; II-1, m. 16), as well as a large number of small-note figures which should be performed as after-notes, taking value from the preceding note and generally to be played in their notated values (e.g., II-1, m. 1; II-3, m. 119).

Improvised Embellishments

While it is assumed that these sonatas, like the other accompanied keyboard sonatas of their day, were written primarily for amateurs' home entertainment, one can also speculate that there was a wide range of ability among those amateurs, who would have embellished them in accordance with their skill. The contemporary duo should proceed accordingly.

Conclusive evidence exists that embellishment of slow movements was a common practice during this period. J. C. Bach and Ricci in 1786 stated that "the performer is at liberty to embellish passages which are often repeated, which are too plain. . . . Nothing demonstrates better the good or bad taste of the musician than his choice of ornaments."[21]

Türk in 1789 offered some guidelines for tasteful embellishment: "It may generally be observed that only those pieces should be varied (but only when the composition is repeated) which would otherwise not be interesting enough and consequently become tedious. . . . Longer elaborations are most frequently used in compositions of a gentle, pleasing character in slow tempo" (p. 311). Variation could be made by adding notes, displacing the rhythm, alternating dynamics, slurring, detaching, or sustaining. Türk's guidelines (pp. 312–13) were as follows: the added embellishments must (1) be appropriate to the character of the composition; (2) be at least as good as the given melody; (3) not be repeated too often; (4) appear easy; (5) not embellish what is already beautiful; (6) not change the tempo; and (7) not change the harmony.

Many pianists apparently must have carried improvisation far beyond these guidelines. Philipp Carl Hoffman published his overly florid embellishments for slow movements of Mozart's last six concertos in 1801 and 1802. Hummel, who was Mozart's student, wrote elaborate and flamboyant embellishments which virtually obliterated the original melody.

Perhaps the best guide to what is "tasteful" can be gained from examination of the written-out embellishments of Mozart in his sonatas and trios. The slow movements of the Sonatas for Piano and Violin, K. 454 and K. 481, and the Piano Trio, K. 502, are excellent examples. Based on these, one can develop some general observations on "appropriate" additions: (1) appoggiaturas may be added; (2) long notes may be filled in with turns or more elaborate figurations; (3) melodic lines may be filled out, but with the original contour and even the exact notes of the line intact or implied; (4) rhythm may be varied, but repetition of identical rhythmic motives should be avoided; and (5) elaboration need not be limited to the melodic line but can be applied to the accompanying part as well.

Pinto's slow movements are melodically sketchy and can benefit greatly from tasteful embellishment, particularly in the repetitions of the themes. The appendix offers a suggested embellishment of I-2, but the performers should feel free to experiment with their own additions.[22]

Another case requiring improvisation by the performer is the *Eingang*, or lead-in, "Mozart's own term for an ornamental passage that leads into a theme." According to Frederick Neumann, it is usually indicated by a fermata and may indicate either an introductory passage to a principal theme (often in a rondo) or a prolongation of the preceding phrase. It usually leads from the dominant to the tonic, is fairly brief, and nonthematic, containing mostly passage work.[23]

Türk stated that fermatas may be played without ornamentation (but should be held) or may be embellished. He gave the following guidelines for embellishment (pp. 290–94): the added material (1) must suit the character of the composition; (2) should be based only on the prescribed harmony (but with passing tones allowed); (3) should not be too long, and is not bound by meter; (4) may be a trill or mordent instead of an elaborate embellishment. Türk further elaborates on the rondo transition, stating that it should be short, incorporate the accidentals of the new key, lead into the proper interval of the upper voice, and correspond to the overall character of the composition.

Clementi wrote (p. 14) that the fermata "renders the *note* longer at pleasure, and in certain cases, the composer expects some embellishments from the performer, but the pause on a *rest* only lengthens, at pleasure, the silence." Again, the written-out *Eingang* in Mozart's sonatas can serve as examples to the performer who wants guidance. These can be found in K. 304 (second movement), K. 526 (third movement), and K. 547 (first movement).

The fermatas in Pinto's second and third sonatas require decisions concerning possible *Eingänge*. In II-3, the fermatas in measures 148 and 290 suggest *Eingänge* by the piano, while those in measures 210 and 214 appear to indicate only pauses, not improvisation opportunities. In III-1, measure 128, an *Eingang* could be played by either instrument. Measures 91 and 188 of III-3 seem to call for piano *Eingänge*, while measure 132, because of the sudden harmonic change, does not require one.

Notes

1. Nicholas Temperley, "George Frederick Pinto," *The Musical Times* 106 (1965): 266.
2. Alexander L. Ringer, "Beethoven and the London Pianoforte School," *The Musical Quarterly* 56 (1970): 754–55; Temperley, "George Frederick Pinto," 270; William S. Newman, *The Sonata Since Beethoven*, 3rd ed. (New York: W. W. Norton, 1983), 569.
3. *The New Grove Dictionary of Music and Musicians*, s.v. "Pinto, George Frederick," by Nicholas Temperley.
4. *Grove's Dictionary of Music and Musicians*, 5th ed., s.v. "Pinto, George Frederick," by Carl Ferdinand Pohl; *Dictionary of Musicians, from the Earliest Ages to the Present Time*, comp. John Sainsbury (London: Sainsbury and Company, 1825), 294; *Baker's Biographical Dictionary of Musicians*, 8th ed., ed. Nicholas Slonimsky (New York: MacMillan, 1992), 141.
5. Temperley, "Pinto, George Frederick."
6. Ringer, "Beethoven and the London Pianoforte School," 754; Nicholas Temperley, *The London Pianoforte School*, vol. 14 (New York: Garland Publications, 1985); Nicholas Temperley, *Musica Brittanica*, vol. 43 (London: Stainer and Bell, 1979).
7. Leon Plantinga, *Clementi: His Life and Music* (London: Oxford University Press, 1977), 186.
8. Sandra P. Rosenblum, *Performance Practices in Classic Piano Music: Their Principles and Applications* (Bloomington: Indiana University Press, 1988), 25.
9. William S. Newman, *The Sonata in the Classic Era*, 3rd ed. (New York: W. W. Norton, 1983), 99.
10. *The New Grove Dictionary of Music and Musicians*, s.v. "Cramer," by Jerald C. Graue.
11. Carl Philipp Emanuel Bach, *Essay on the True Art of Playing Keyboard Instruments (1752)*, trans. and ed. William J. Mitchell

(New York: W. W. Norton, 1949), 157; Daniel Gottlob Türk, *School of Clavier Playing (1789),* trans. and ed. Raymond Haggh (Lincoln: University of Nebraska Press, 1982), 345; Friedrich Wilhelm Marpurg's *Anleitung zum Clavierspielen* is cited in Rosenblum, *Performance Practices in Classic Piano Music,* 149.

12. Muzio Clementi, *Introduction to the Art of Playing on the Pianoforte (1801)* (New York: Da Capo Press, 1974), 9; Rosenblum, *Performance Practices in Classic Piano Music,* 154.

13. Leopold Mozart, *A Treatise on the Fundamental Principles of Violin Playing (1756),* trans. Edith Knocker (London: Oxford University Press, 1948), 124.

14. Johann Joachim Quantz, *On Playing the Flute (1752),* trans. Edward R. Reilly (New York: The Free Press, 1966), 232.

15. David D. Boyden, "The Violin and Its Technique in the 18th Century," *The Musical Quarterly* 36 (1950): 14.

16. Ibid., 14.

17. Rosenblum, *Performance Practices in Classic Piano Music,* 63.

18. Ibid., 119.

19. Ibid., 315.

20. Ibid., 314.

21. Johann Christian Bach and Francesco-Pasquale Ricci, *Méthode ou recueil de connoissances élémentaires pour le forte-piano ou clavecin (Paris, 1786)* (Geneva: Minkoff Reprint, 1974), 9–10.

22. For other suggested embellishments, see Linda W. Perry, "An Edition of Three Sonatas for the Pianoforte with an Accompaniment for a Violin by George Frederick Pinto" (D.M.A. diss., University of Illinois, 1994).

23. Frederick Neumann, *Ornamentation and Improvisation in Mozart* (Princeton: Princeton University Press, 1989), 264.

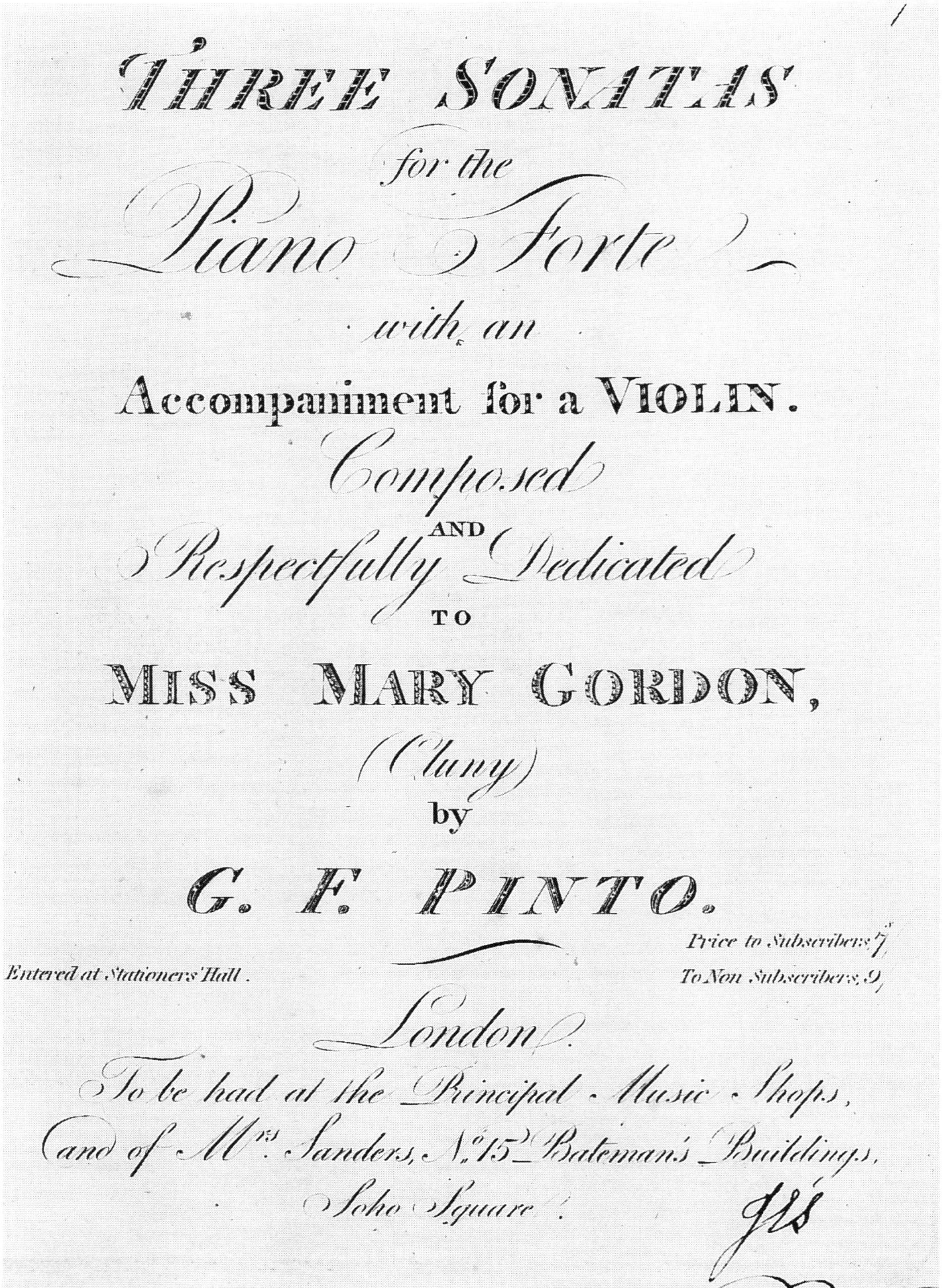

THREE SONATAS
for the
Piano Forte
with an
Accompaniment for a VIOLIN.
Composed
AND
Respectfully Dedicated
TO
MISS MARY GORDON,
(Cluny)
by
G. F. PINTO.

Entered at Stationers' Hall.

Price to Subscribers 7s.
To Non Subscribers 9s.

London.
To be had at the Principal Music Shops,
and of Mrs. Sanders, No. 15 Bateman's Buildings,
Soho Square.

Plate 1. George Frederick Pinto, *Three Sonatas for the Pianoforte with an Accompaniment for a Violin* (London, 1806), title page. Courtesy of Nicholas Temperley.

Plate 2. George Frederick Pinto, *Three Sonatas for the Pianoforte with an Accompaniment for a Violin* (London, 1806), Sonata No. 1 in G Minor, first page of piano part. Courtesy of Nicholas Temperley.

Plate 3. George Frederick Pinto, *Three Sonatas for the Pianoforte with an Accompaniment for a Violin* (London, 1806), Sonata No. 1 in G Minor, first page of violin part. Courtesy of Nicholas Temperley.

Sonata No. 1 in G Minor

Allegro moderato con espressione

14

Sonata No. 2 in A Major

Allegro moderato con espressione

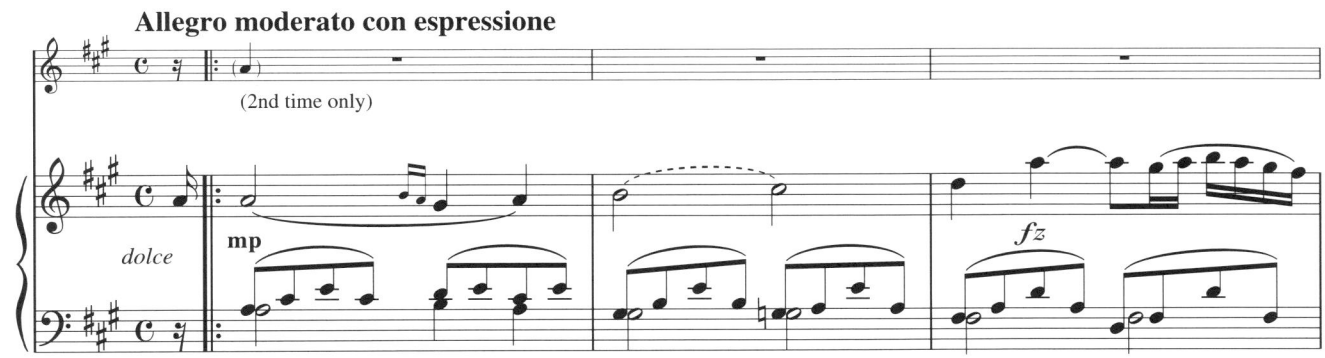

* See critical note.

57

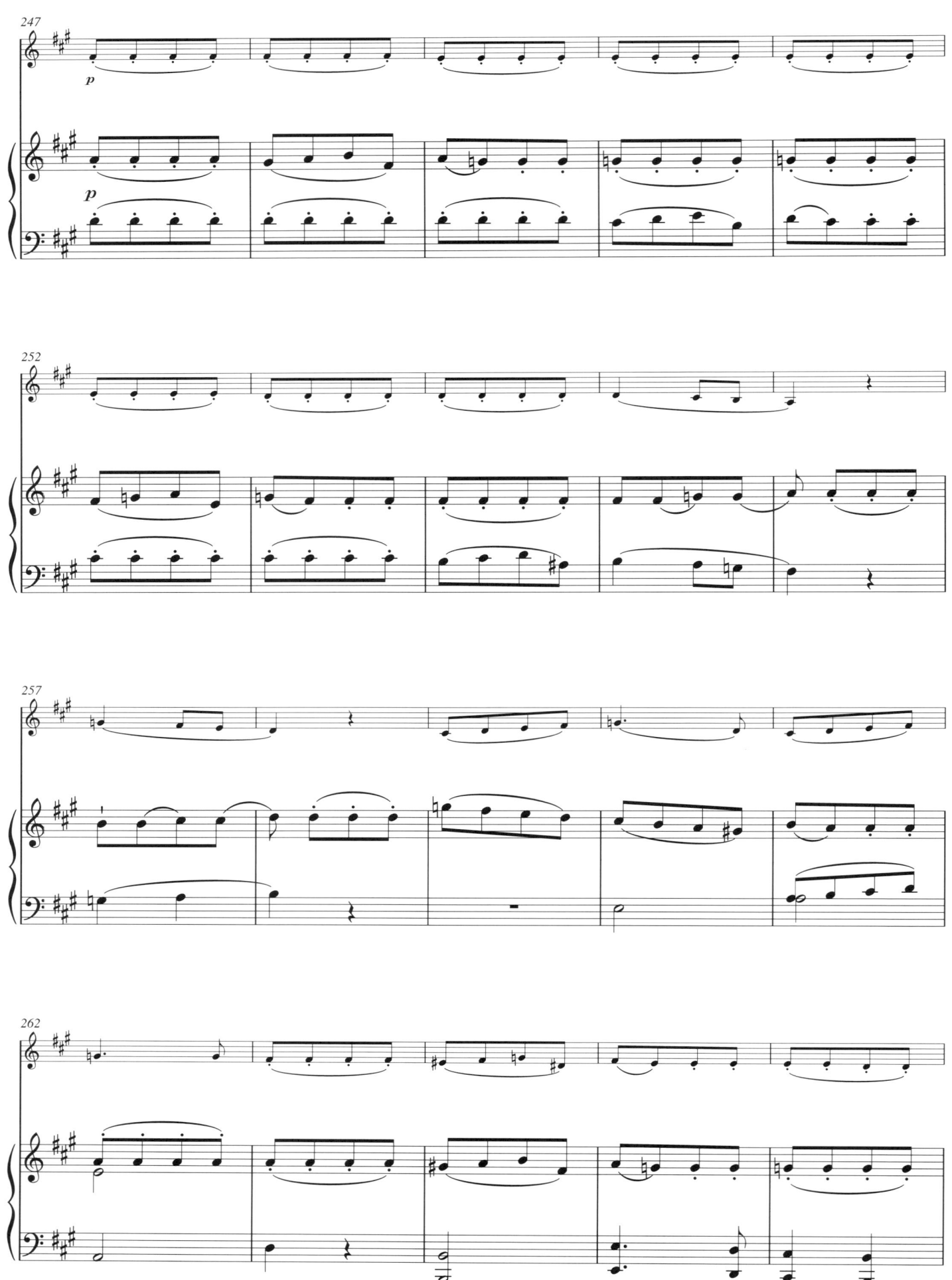

Sonata No. 3 in B-flat Major

Rondo: Allegro moderato
Pastorale e legato

90

Critical Report

Source

The source for this edition was a microfilm from the British Library (h.1480.s) of the sole publication in 1806 by Mrs. Saunders, Pinto's mother. The piano and violin parts were printed separately, with no full score. The plates used in this edition were photographed from a copy in the personal collection of Dr. Nicholas Temperley.

Editorial Methods

A piano and violin score has been compiled, modernizing the notation somewhat for easier reading. Full titles for the sonatas have been provided (rather than the "Sonata I," etc., of the source); movement titles are regularized with any abbreviations written out. Whereas Pinto frequently wrote the right hand notes on the lower staff, everything played by the right hand has been assigned to the upper staff, changing the clef signs when necessary. The notation has been aligned vertically. Stemming, beaming, and slurring have been modernized for consistency. Slur markings indicating groupettes rather than phrasing have been tacitly removed. Slashes have been removed from turn signs. Accidentals that are redundant by modern standards have been tacitly removed except in cases where they are useful as cautionaries. Editorially added cautionaries are placed in parentheses; other editorial accidentals are placed in brackets.

Pinto's casual placement of articulation and dynamic markings is evident throughout. Samuel Wesley, editing Pinto's Fantasia and Sonata after his death, diplomatically describes his manner of writing (quoted in Nicholas Temperley, *The London Pianoforte School*, vol. 14 [New York: Garland Publications, 1985], 111):

> They who know the author's mode of committing his musical ideas to paper, must remember, that he always produced them with remarkable rapidity (*currente calamo*), and consequently, that as he scarcely ever corrected the original copy, there must sometimes happen some trifling inaccuracies, which, although never of sufficient importance to disfigure or disgrace his page, much less to destroy or injure its general good effect, yet might possibly excite the hypercritical remarks of those who are unwilling to admit the smallest deviation from the strict rules of ancient composition.

No attempt has been made to reconcile all these inconsistencies. However, articulation, slurring, and dynamic patterns have been regularized between obviously parallel passages or as called for by context. Added slurs, ties, and hairpins are dashed; added letter dynamics are set in bold type rather than the customary bold-italic; all other added markings and indications are placed in brackets.

Critical Notes

The notes below describe rejected source readings. The following abbreviations are used: Vn. = Violin; Pn. = Piano; r.h. = right hand; l.h. = left hand; m(m). = measure(s). Notes are numbered consecutively within a measure; notes sounding simultaneously are numbered from bottom to top. Where appropriate, chords are numbered rather than specific notes. Pitches are indicated by the system in which middle C = c'.

Sonata No. 1 in G Minor

Allegro moderato con espressione

Mm. 17–19, Pn., articulations are dots. M. 47, Pn., l.h., note 1 is double-dotted eighth note. M. 57, Vn., note 7 has stroke. M. 82, Pn., r.h., notes 1–2 are dotted quarter notes; note 3 is eighth note. M. 104, Pn., r.h., note 17, parentheses on ♮ are original to source. Mm. 106–7, Pn., r.h. and l.h., slur to m. 107, note 1. M. 128, Pn., *sf* on beat 1. M. 143, Pn., r.h. and l.h., chord 1 has dotted-quarter value, chord 2 has eighth value. Mm. 146, 148, and 150, Vn., note has *tr*. M. 158, Vn. has *lento* (not in m. 161). Mm. 162 and 163, Pn., r.h., note 2 is double-dotted quarter note, note 3 is sixteenth note.

Adagio

Mm. 3 and 12, Pn., r.h., note 1 is double-dotted quarter note. M. 11, Vn., note 1 is double-dotted quarter note. Mm. 24 and 26, Pn., articulations are strokes. M. 73, Vn., articulations are strokes.

Rondo: Allegretto grazioso

Mm. 13–14, Pn., r.h., slur to m. 14, chord 1; l.h., slur to m. 14, note 1. M. 79, Pn., r.h., note 1 has slash. Mm. 81 and 87, Pn., l.h., note 1 has slash. M. 132, Vn., note 2 has *tr*. M. 148, Pn., l.h., note 2 is b♭. Mm. 149 and 151, Vn., note 1 has ∞. M. 185, Pn., l.h., note 1 is e.

Sonata No. 2 in A Major

Allegro moderato con espressione

Common pattern of tied notes followed by slurred notes (see m. 3, Pn., r.h.) usually has slur beginning after tie; all have been regularized to that pattern. M. 36, Pn., r.h., note 4 is dotted eighth note, note 5 is sixteenth note. Mm. 70–75, Pn., r.h. is sporadically marked with dots and strokes.

Andante

Slurs, dots, and strokes are used inconsistently throughout; all conflicting notations have been emended to slurred dots, since a mezzo-staccato interpretation seems preferable in this movement. M. 52, c#' in the violin creates an unlikely dissonance with the piano and should perhaps be preceded by an appoggiatura on d' to match the lower line in the piano's right hand.

Rondo: Allegro con brio

The repeated staccato notes of the principal theme are marked inconsistently throughout the movement, occurring first as strokes, later as dots or slurred dots; all have been emended to strokes. Mm. 24–25, Vn., slur to m. 25, note 1. M. 41, Vn., note is b'. M. 76, Vn. has *f* under note 1 and *p* under note 2 (not in m. 75). M. 82, Vn. lacks measure. M. 121, Pn., r.h., eighth rest precedes chord 2. M. 151, Vn. has fermata (not in m. 148). Mm. 151–52, Pn., l.h., slur to m. 152, note 1. Mm. 172–73, Vn., slur to m. 173, note 1; Pn., r.h., slur to m. 173, chord 1. M. 198, Vn. and Pn., numeral "1" indicates resting bar. M. 239, Pn., l.h., slur on notes 1–3. M. 291, Vn. has fermata (not in m. 290). Mm. 293–94, Pn., l.h., slur to m. 294, note 1. Mm. 310–11, Pn., l.h., slur to m. 311, note 1.

Sonata No. 3 in B-flat Major

Allegro moderato con espressione con spirito

M. 3, Pn., r.h., notes 1–2; m. 4, Vn., notes 1–2; etc.: quarter notes in first theme notated with various articulations in parallel situations throughout the movement; all have been emended to slurred dots. M. 11, Pn., r.h., note 3 is dotted quarter note, note 4 is eighth note. M. 124, Pn., r.h., note 4 is e♭'. M. 136, Pn., r.h., note 10 is lacking. M. 137, Pn., r.h., note 2 is lacking. M. 139, Pn., r.h., note 5 is dotted quarter note, note 6 is eighth note. M. 165, Pn., chord 1 has *ff* (not in m. 164). M. 180, Vn., notes 4–5 are eighth notes.

Adagio affettuoso e con sentimento

M. 57, Vn., note 2 is dotted eighth note, note 3 is sixteenth note. M. 71, Pn., l.h., note 3 lacks augmentation dot. M. 86, Pn., l.h., chord has quarter value followed by single eighth rest.

Rondo: Allegro moderato

Slurring of opening four-note figure inconsistent throughout the movement, with the four notes slurred, unslurred, or slurred through one or both following eighth notes; all have been emended to four-note slurs. Mm. 2, 4, Pn., r.h.; mm. 10, 12, Vn.; etc.: in these and parallel passages, slurs are sometimes marked and sometimes are not; no attempt has been made to regularize the practice. M. 88, Pn., r.h., note 1 is f. M. 105, Pn., r.h., note 1 is lacking. M. 117, Pn., r.h., note 4 is c', note 5 is e♭'. M. 156, Pn., r.h., note 7 is a#.

Appendix

An Embellished Version of the Adagio of Sonata No. 1

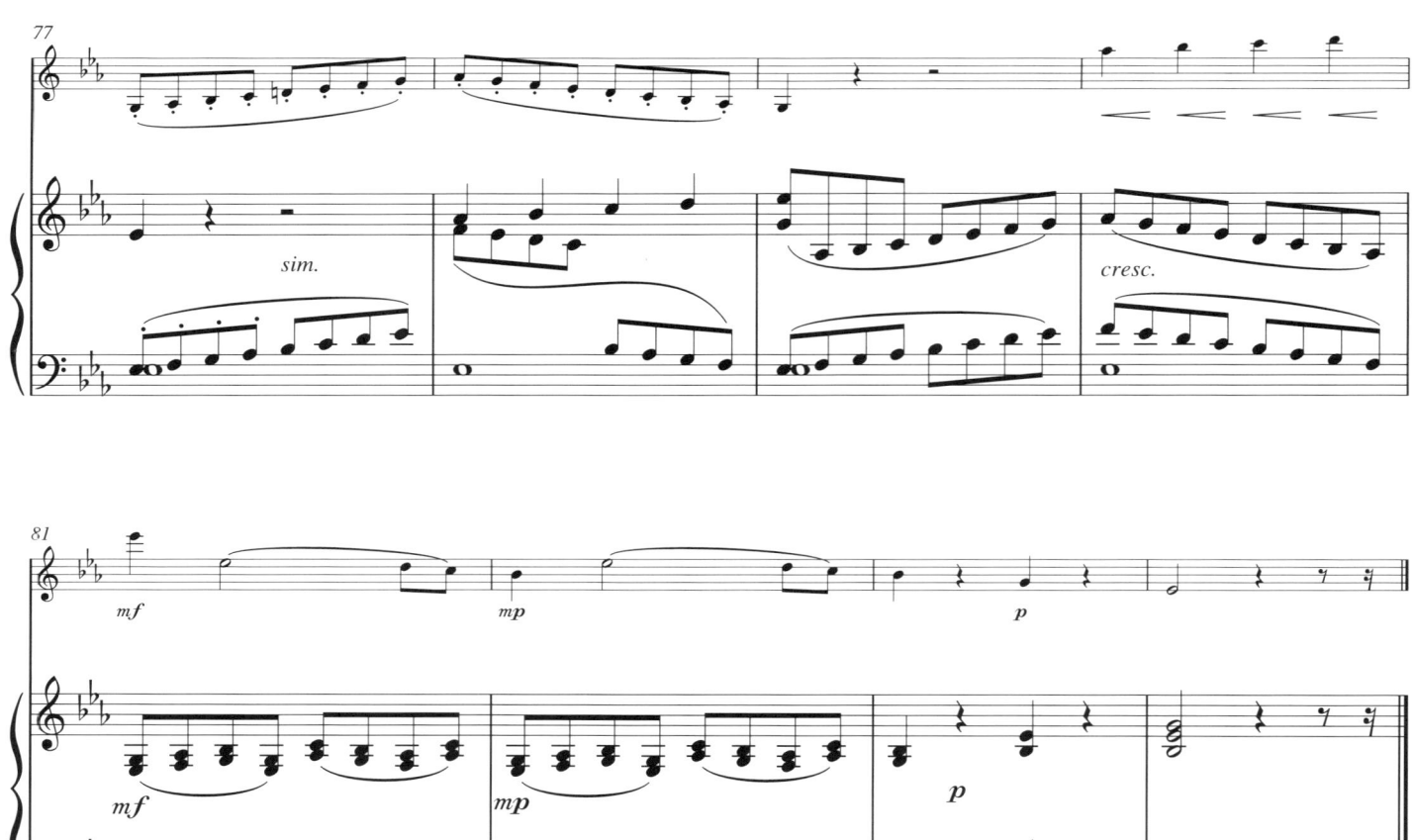

Recent Researches in the Music of the Nineteenth and
Early Twentieth Centuries
Rufus Hallmark, general editor

Vol.	Composer: *Title*
1–2	Jan Ladislav Dussek: *Selected Piano Works*
3–4	Johann Nepomuk Hummel: *Piano Concerto, Opus 113*
5	*One Hundred Years of Eichendorff Songs*
6	Etienne-Nicolas Méhul: *Symphony No. 1 in G Minor*
7–8	*Embellished Opera Arias*
9	*The Nineteenth-Century Piano Ballade: An Anthology*
10	*Famous Poets, Neglected Composers: Songs to Lyrics by Goethe, Heine, Mörike, and Others*
11	Charles-Marie Widor: *Symphonie I in C Minor*
12	Charles-Marie Widor: *Symphonie II in D Major*
13	Charles-Marie Widor: *Symphonie III in E Minor*
14	Charles-Marie Widor: *Symphonie IV in F Minor*
15	Charles-Marie Widor: *Symphonie V in F Minor*
16	Charles-Marie Widor: *Symphonie VI in G Minor*
17	Charles-Marie Widor: *Symphonie VII in A Minor*
18	Charles-Marie Widor: *Symphonie VIII in B Major*
19	Charles-Marie Widor: *Symphonie gothique*
20	Charles-Marie Widor: *Symphonie romane*
21	Archduke Rudolph of Austria: *Forty Variations on a Theme by Beethoven for Piano; Sonata in F Minor for Violin and Piano*
22	Fanny Hensel: *Songs for Pianoforte, 1836–1837*
23	*Anthology of Goethe Songs*
24	Walter Rabl: *Complete Instrumental Chamber Works*
25	Stefano Pavesi: *Dies irae concertato*
26	Franz Liszt: *St. Stanislaus*
27	George Frederick Pinto: *Three Sonatas for Pianoforte with Violin*